Allen Creek Elementary
6505 60th DR NE
Marysville, WA 98270

HISTORIC
COMMUNITIES

TRAVEL
in the Early Days

Bobbie Kalman and Kate Calder

Crabtree Publishing Company

www.crabtreebooks.com

HISTORIC COMMUNITIES

Created by Bobbie Kalman

To Heather Levigne
from across the hall

Editor-in-Chief
Bobbie Kalman

Writing team
Bobbie Kalman
Kate Calder

Managing editor
Lynda Hale

Editors
Niki Walker
Hannelore Sotzek
John Crossingham
Amanda Bishop

Computer design
Lynda Hale

Production coordinator
Hannelore Sotzek

Special thanks to
Black Creek Pioneer Village / TRCA

Photographs
Black Creek Pioneer Village / TRCA: pages 10 (both), 11 (all)

Illustrations and reproductions
Valérie Apprioual: pages 3 (teamboat), 6 (middle and bottom), 7 (bottom); Barbara Bedell: cover (inset), title page, pages 3 (all except boats), 8, 12-13, 16, 17, 22, 23 (top), 25, 26 (bottom), 27, 28, 29, 30; Antoinette "Cookie" Bortolon: page 6 (top); ©Crabtree Publishing Company: pages 26, 31 (bottom); Currier & Ives: page 24; John Mantha: back cover; Jeannette McNaughton-Julich: page 31 (top); Janet Newey: page 9 (bottom); Bonna Rouse: pages 3 (keelboat), 5 (bottom), 7 (top and middle), 9 (top), 12 (top), 14, 15, 19; other images by Digital Stock and Eyewire, Inc.

Digital prepress
Best Graphics Int'l Co.; Embassy Graphics (cover)

Printer
Worzalla Publishing Company

Crabtree Publishing Company

www.crabtreebooks.com   1-800-387-7650

PMB 16A
350 Fifth Ave.,
Suite 3308
New York, NY
10118

612 Welland Ave.
St. Catharines,
Ontario,
Canada
L2M 5V6

73 Lime Walk
Headington
Oxford
0X3 7AD
United Kingdom

Cataloging-in-Publication Data
Kalman, Bobbie
   Travel in the early days

p. cm. — (Historic communities)
Includes index.

ISBN 0-86505-442-8 (library bound) — ISBN 0-86505-472-X (pbk.)
This book introduces readers to transportation used by settlers in North America. Topics include covered wagons, canal boats, steam power, and hazards that early travelers faced.

1. Transportation—North America—History—Juvenile literature.
[1. Transportation—History.] I. Calder, Kate. II. Title. III. Series: Kalman, Bobbie. Historic communities.

HE151 .K323 2001   j388' .0973—dc21   LC00-034609
                                                                                CIP

Contents

Travel in a new land

Modern travel is quick and simple. Roads, cars, trains, and airplanes make it easy to get from place to place. In the past, however, travel was slow, difficult, and often dangerous. When the first explorers reached North America, they faced rough land, thick forests, and raging rivers. These adventurers did not journey far from major waterways such as rivers and lakes.

Canoe travel

About two hundred years after the first explorers arrived, the fur trade was thriving in North America. Hundreds of traders came in search of wealth. They traded with the Native Americans, who traveled in small, lightweight boats called **canoes**. Trappers and fur traders quickly adopted this important means of travel. Now they could travel deep inland along shallow rivers and streams where larger boats could not go. Some canoes were big enough to transport sixty people as well as supplies, equipment, and furs. Smaller canoes could be **portaged**, or lifted and carried across land from one waterway to another.

Over land

On land, the first settlers followed trails made by Native Americans. Travelers also **blazed** trails of their own. Blazed trails were marked by cuts made in trees with a **hatchet**. These trails kept people from getting lost. Marked trails also connected settlements that developed inland. Most new settlers traveled on foot and walked many miles over rough, forested land to reach the next town. Wild animals made the journey even more threatening.

No bridges

Explorers traveling inland were unaware of all the rivers and lakes that crisscrossed the land. Many travelers came across large bodies of water. There were no bridges, so they often had to walk for hours to find a shallow spot where they could wade across. Some people made temporary bridges by laying long tree trunks across rivers.

(top) Native Americans showed hunters and trappers how to build birch-bark canoes.

(right) In the winter, hunters and trappers trudged through the deep snow with snowshoes, which kept them from sinking.

On the water

Dugouts *were boats made from large tree trunks. The trunks were hollowed out and chiseled to form a canoe.*

Waterways were crucial to the early settlers because shipments of supplies from Europe arrived by boat. Settlements and farms were established along rivers and lakes so that people, tools, food, and other goods could be transported easily from place to place. Settlers built a variety of boats for traveling on lakes and rivers. They used paddles, sails, poles, and horses to move the boats through water.

bateau

Bateaux

Bateaux were long narrow boats with large sails. When there was no wind to fill the sails and move the bateau, passengers had to push the boat along with poles or paddles. Trappers and traders transported their furs to towns and cities by bateaux. Many settler families also traveled on these boats. When night fell, the boat was **docked**, or tied to shore. The passengers camped nearby or slept at a hotel if there was one in the area.

flatboat

Flatboats

Flatboats were large, wide boats with a flat bottom for traveling on shallow rivers. They used the river's **current**, or flow, to float along. A large oar at the back of the boat steered it left or right. People stored their belongings in the cabin, which also provided a place to sleep and eat. Some families lived on their flatboat for months while they traveled down a river. When they arrived at the site of their new home, they used the boat as their temporary shelter until they could build a house.

keelboat

Keelboats

Keelboats were long boats with points at both the front and back. Settlers used these boats to travel upstream against the current. A large **keel** ran along the bottom of the boat. It protected the **hull** against logs or rocks that were under water. Keelboats had a sail to power the boat with wind. If there was no wind, the passengers pushed the boat using poles. They walked on the deck along wooden rungs, which allowed them to dig in their heels for extra pushing power. Often one passenger played a fiddle while the others pushed to the beat of the music.

Canal boats

Artificial waterways known as **canals** were constructed for traveling in areas where rivers were too rough for travel or where rivers did not flow. **Canal boats** were long boats that had a large, flat-topped cabin. Some of the passengers sat on top of the cabin as the boat moved along the canal. Mules or horses were attached by a rope and pulled the boat along from the shore. Sometimes several families lived on a canal boat while they traveled to their new home.

canal boat

Horse power

Teamboats used horses to move the boat forward. The horses were placed in booths on each side of the boat. When the horses walked, they caused a large wheel under the deck to turn. The wheel was attached to an **axle**, which turned paddles. The paddles pushed the boat through the water. Most teamboats were used as **ferries** to carry people across rivers. Without bridges, ferries were the only way settlers could cross some deep, wide rivers.

teamboat

Roads and wagons

Some settlers brought horses and oxen with them from Europe to North America. These animals were bred by the settlers and became plentiful in the new land. The settlers depended on horses and oxen to transport them and their belongings from place to place. These animals were also used in the fields to clear the land and plant and harvest crops.

Important animals

Animals were very valuable to the settlers. If a horse or ox was stolen, settlers were often left stranded and were unable to move heavy loads. In many places it was a serious crime to steal horses, and thieves were often hanged.

Wagons, carts, and carriages

Settlers also used carts and wagons to travel and to transport supplies. Simple carts were made of wooden boxes attached to wheels. Wagons were larger than carts and were used to carry people as well as supplies. Often two or more animals pulled a wagon. Horse-drawn carriages were lighter and fancier than wagons. A seat in a carriage was more comfortable because it was used only for carrying people.

Animals were attached with long poles to carts, wagons, and carriages. This settler uses his oxen to carry heavy loads. He steers them as they pull a cart full of logs for firewood.

Bumpy roads

Eventually, most of the land along waterways was settled, so new settlers had to establish their farms farther inland. The foot trails leading inland were too narrow for wagons. Over time, settlers widened these trails by cutting down the trees on either side. The trails easily became rutted and muddy with constant travel. To solve this problem, settlers split logs and laid them across the path to make a **corduroy road**. Corduroy roads were very bumpy. Horses often hurt their legs when their hoofs slipped between the logs.

Toll roads

After a **sawmill** was built in an area, people began making roads with flat boards called **planks**. Plank roads were much smoother than corduroy roads. In some places, the roads were built by companies. The company that owned the road charged people a **toll**, or fee, for traveling on it. Tollgate keepers were hired to collect fees from travelers. The fees were supposed to be used for repairing the road, but many roads were in poor condition.

(above) Corduroy roads kept settlers from getting stuck in the mud, but they made traveling bumpy and uncomfortable.

This couple has stopped at the tollgate to pay their fee, but many travelers tried to race past the toll collector without paying.

Travel tradespeople

Most settlers used their wagon or cart for both transportation and hauling goods to and from town. Very few people had the skills needed to make or repair their vehicles, so tradespeople such as blacksmiths, **farriers**, and **wheelwrights** set up workshops in towns. Settlers paid these artisans to fix broken wagons and make the supplies used for traveling.

The blacksmith

Horses, oxen, and mules needed metal shoes to protect the bottom of their hoofs. The blacksmith made U-shaped horseshoes out of iron. He heated a piece of iron in a large brick fireplace called a **forge** until the black metal turned white or yellow. The hot iron was easily cut and shaped with a hammer. The blacksmith then dipped the hot shoe into a barrel of water to cool and harden.

The harness maker

Settlers needed harnesses and straps to attach animals to wagons and control their movements. The harness maker was a skilled leather worker who sold new saddles and harnesses. He or she also repaired damaged equipment.

The farrier

A farrier **shod**, or attached, horseshoes to a horse's hoofs. He first removed damaged or worn-out horseshoes. Next, he used metal tools to clean dirt from the bottom of the hoofs. Then he filed the hoofs smooth so the shoes would fit snugly. Finally, the farrier hammered the shoes directly onto the bottom of the hoofs. He used small nails, which did not hurt the animals. Many farriers also treated wounded and diseased horses.

The blacksmith heated iron white-hot in order to shape it into horseshoes.

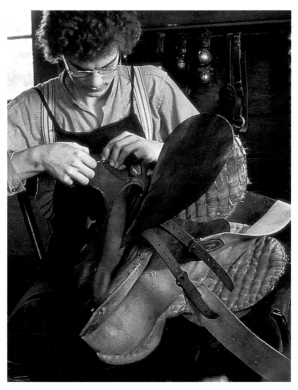

The harness maker made saddles, harnesses, and whips out of leather.

The wheelwright made and repaired wheels. The first wagon wheels were made entirely of wood. In later times, the wheelwright attached metal tires to the rims to make the wheels last longer.

Some blacksmiths were also farriers. This blacksmith files the horse's hoofs to keep them healthy and strong.

The **wainwright** made wagons and carriages for the townspeople.

Gliding over snow

When winter arrived, the harsh, cold weather required changes in the modes of transportation. Deep snow on the trails made walking impossible, and wagon wheels often got stuck. Water froze, so people could not travel by boat on rivers and lakes. To cope with winter, settlers found new ways to get around on ice and snow.

Traveling on foot

Some settlers used snowshoes to walk on snow. Others strapped long strips of wood to their boots. Settlers used these "skis" to glide over the snow. They pushed themselves along with long poles.

Sleighs

Instead of wagons and carts, people traveled in **sleighs** in the winter. Sleighs were similar to carts, but they had no wheels. Two flat metal bars called **runners** slid easily over snow. Sleighs came in different shapes and sizes. Some were plain wagons, but others were fancy. **Cutters** were small sleighs that were pulled by a single horse. Some settlers traveled on a small sled pulled by a team of dogs.

Snowshoes were wide wooden frames with leather netting. They were strapped onto boots.

Rivers and lakes were not an obstacle in winter. The thick ice made it easy for travelers to glide over them. This winter stagecoach has runners instead of wheels.

Time for fun

During the winter months, people finally had some free time to enjoy themselves. The settlers did not have to tend their crops, and autumn chores such as preserving food and grinding grain were completed. They used this opportunity to visit friends, especially during the Christmas holiday season. To make their sleighs more festive, people attached bells and ribbons to the bridles of their horses. The bells acted as a signal to other travelers that a sleigh was coming. The expression, "I'll be there with bells on" means "I'm looking forward to visiting you!"

*(above) People kept warm on a sleigh by covering themselves with fur blankets. Sometimes they put **foot warmers** on the floor. Foot warmers were metal boxes filled with hot coals.*

13

Winter hazards

Winter travel was usually comfortable and quick. Gliding over snow was a happy change from bumpy rides in wagons and coaches. Sleighs slid smoothly over stumps, ruts, and rocks that lay buried deep under snow. Snow travel could be risky, however. Speedy drivers often lost control of their sleigh. Large, steep snowdrifts also caused sleighs to overturn or get stuck.

Blizzards

Blizzards were a winter traveler's greatest fear. People who were outdoors during a blizzard could quickly freeze to death. Travelers caught in sudden snowstorms sometimes lost their way and became stranded. They could do little but huddle together with their animals for warmth while waiting for the storm to end.

Feeling the way

Thick snow and driving wind could be so blinding that settlers sometimes got lost on their own farm! To find their way in snowstorms, people tied a rope between their house and barn. During blizzards, they held onto the rope and used it to guide them from one building to another.

On thin ice

Traveling over ice that was not frozen solid was extremely dangerous. Large areas of thin ice were often hidden under a fresh blanket of snow. If the ice cracked and broke, the driver had to act quickly. He or she tied a rope around the horse's neck to keep the animal's head above water and then pulled on the rope to help the horse to safety.

These settlers have had a freezing surprise.
Their sleigh was too heavy for the ice.

Stagecoaches

In the mid-1700s, **stagecoaches** were a common mode of transportation. Stagecoaches were carriages that took people from town to town. Travelers were charged a fee according to how far they were traveling. At some stops the driver changed horses. These carriages were called stagecoaches because the distance between stops was known as a **stage** of the journey.

This village has stables for sheltering horses. There is a tavern where people can buy a meal or spend the night while the stagecoach stops to change horses. Which jobs are being done by the coachmen at this stage stop? Examine the picture and name four tasks.

Tough going

Many stagecoaches were uncomfortable. They were small, cramped, and provided a bumpy ride. Passengers sat inside the carriage, on the front bench with the driver, or even on top of the coach. Stagecoaches were unsteady on the rough roads and sometimes tipped over. Passengers often had to lean to one side to make sure the coach stayed upright!

Dangerous drivers

A stagecoach driver was known as a **coachman**. Some coachmen were reckless drivers who tried to reach the next town as quickly as possible. The faster they finished a trip, the sooner they could start another one and make more money. They turned corners sharply and sped along dangerously with little care for the comfort or safety of their passengers.

Mail carriers

Some stagecoaches carried mail as well as passengers. Every week, mail was collected from and delivered to general stores along the stagecoach route. Bandits often robbed stagecoaches that carried mail because many letters contained money.

This stagecoach is caught in a winter storm. Riding on top of the cabin is cold, but the coachman continues to forge ahead.

This stagecoach is heading out of town on a Sunday sightseeing trip. In the summer, sightseeing trips were a popular pastime.

17

Wagon trains

In the mid-1800s, many settlers left eastern towns and cities to seek new opportunities in the West. They began their long journey in April or May and took several months to reach their destination. Harsh weather, wild animals, fast-flowing rivers, and steep, rocky mountain passes made the trip difficult and dangerous. There was also the risk of injury and disease. Settlers traveled in a long **convoy**, or group, of many wagons known as a **wagon train**. Being in a wagon train provided protection and support for the long journey.

Covered wagons

Settlers transported their possessions in a **covered wagon**. They stretched a canvas **tarpaulin**, or cover, over a wooden frame to protect the contents of the wagon. Early covered wagons were called **Conestoga wagons**. They were used for transporting supplies and traveling between towns. As people started traveling great distances to the West, they built covered wagons that were bigger and sturdier for the long distances across the plains and mountains.

Prairie schooners

The settlers called the covered wagons **prairie schooners** after a type of sailing ship called a **schooner**. From a distance, a wagon's white cover looked like a ship's sail. Large wheels lifted the wagon high off the ground so it would not hit rocks or stumps along the path. The distance between the wagon and the ground also helped when crossing a river. If the water was too deep, the settlers removed the wheels and floated the wagon across the river like a raft.

No free rides

The wagon was fully packed with the family's supplies which made it very heavy. The driver sat on a bench at the front of the wagon, and others walked alongside to make it easier for the animals to pull. Only small children or sick family members rode inside.

Wagon trains traveled through all types of harsh weather, including thunderstorms. The travelers could not afford to stop, even in very stormy weather. They had a long way to go and wanted to complete the trip before winter. They did not want to be caught in a deadly blizzard!

Western travel

Most of the West was unsettled wilderness with no roads. Horses were essential for travel and work in the West. Many people mined for gold or worked on cattle ranches. Miners relied on horses to carry supplies long distances. Cowboys rode horses to round up cattle and **drive**, or guide, them to market. Horses were also needed to pull stagecoaches carrying travelers.

Western coaches

Traveling west in a stagecoach was tiring. Passengers often rode all night through the vast wilderness. The few hotels along the trail were uncomfortable and dirty. They had thin walls made of canvas, and travelers slept on mattresses of flour sacks stuffed with straw. Coaches stopped for short breaks at **ranchos**, which were small taverns with dirt floors.

Stagecoaches in the West were even less comfortable than those in the East. Western passengers faced long and difficult journeys over rough, dusty trails.

*Before ranchers and miners began settling in the West, herds of wild horses roamed the land. Mexican cowboys, called **vaqueros**, caught many of these wild horses and tamed them. They taught the cowboys from the eastern towns how to tame horses and herd and rope cattle.*

The Wild West

Many criminals moved west because there were few sheriffs. Criminals made travel difficult and even dangerous. Travelers feared attacks from bandits on the long, lonely trails. Thieves often stole settlers' possessions such as clothing, tools, money, and even their horses! This lawless land became known as the "Wild West."

Traveling on horseback was the cheapest and quickest way to travel. The horses became accustomed to walking over the steep, rocky land in mountainous areas and on the hot, dry sand in the deserts.

Traveling by stagecoach was risky. Outlaws often stopped coaches along the trails and robbed the passengers of their money and jewelry.

*Western women did not ride **sidesaddle**, as women riders did in the East. They straddled the horse, making riding much easier.*

In the city

As cities grew, the sidewalks became crowded with people and the streets bustled with wagons, carriages, and stagecoaches. Sometimes the streets were so crowded with traffic that it was difficult to get anywhere! Streetcars and bicycles were common modes of transportation in the city.

Bicycles

Many people began riding bicycles in the late 1800s. Riding a bicycle was quicker than walking and did not require a horse. The first bicycles were called **penny farthings**. They had a huge front wheel on which the seat was placed, making it difficult to get on and off. Eventually, penny farthings were replaced by bicycles with two even-sized wheels.

The tires of penny farthings were made of metal hoops, which were easily bent and damaged by ruts or rocks on the road.

*The **hansom cab** was named after its designer, Joseph Hansom. The passengers of this carriage gave instructions to the driver through a trap door in the roof.*

Large wooden carriages carried passengers through the city streets.

Streetcars

Early streetcars were large coaches pulled by horses. Later streetcars traveled along metal tracks that were built into the roads. They were pulled by a team of horses or mules. The cars had a roof, but often the sides had open windows, so the passengers got wet and cold when it rained or snowed. Passengers paid a small fee to ride the streetcars. The driver stopped to pick up passengers at any point along the route. To request a stop, they signaled the driver by pulling on a string that was attached to his foot.

Sometimes a streetcar ran off the tracks. In order to continue on their journey, the passengers had to get out and help put the car back on the tracks.

Sunday drivers

On Sundays, many people dressed in their finest clothes and took carriage rides through the city. The horses were well-groomed, and the carriages were polished and shiny. Sunday drives allowed people to show off their best clothes, horses, and carriages.

Those who could not afford to own a fine team of horses or a shiny carriage, such as the one in this picture, watched those who could. This handsome couple is getting a lot of attention! People stop and stare, wishing they could ride in such a fine carriage and wear such beautiful clothes.

Steam engines allowed people to travel faster and easier than ever before. The steamboats in this picture had a paddle wheel on either side of the boat. Others had a single paddle wheel at the back.

Steam power

The invention of the steam engine changed the way people traveled. In the early 1800s, steam engines were designed to power boats and trains. A steam engine is fueled by burning coal or wood. The heat from this fire boils water, creating steam. The steam builds up in a closed container and creates a lot of pressure. When the steam is released from the container, its force moves wheels inside the engine. As these wheels turn, they also force the wheels of the vehicle to turn.

The first steamboats

Steamboats used steam engines to turn giant paddle wheels, which pushed the boats through water. Some steamboats had sails so they could also use the wind for power. The first steamboats were unstable and uncomfortable. The bouncy, rocking motion of the boat made many passengers ill. Steamboat captains also enjoyed racing them against other boats, adding to the passengers' rough ride. Racing could overheat the engine and create too much steam, causing the engine to explode.

Popular way to travel

Soon, bigger and better steamboats were built. They were safer and much more comfortable for long journeys. Steamboats became a popular means of travel and were used to ship goods such as sugar, cattle, and cotton to various cities.

Many steamboats were luxurious. They had beautiful furniture, carpeting, and fine china. Musicians were often hired to entertain the guests. Some steamboats even had a casino on board where people could gamble.

The railroad

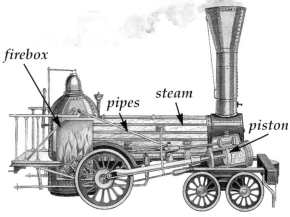

In the early locomotives, water boiled to steam in metal pipes. The pipes were heated by a wood fire in a firebox. The pressure from the steam moved a piston back and forth, which turned the wheels.

firebox

pipes

steam

piston

Steam engines called **locomotives** pulled trains. The building of the first locomotives was part of an experiment in the early 1800s. People wanted to see if a cart could be powered by a steam engine. Before long, people built locomotives with cars for carrying passengers and goods. The first railroads linked large eastern cities. This new and fast method of travel became popular, and railway tracks soon spread westward. In later years, many people traveled by rail to settle new areas all over North America.

Building the railroad

Building railroads was slow, backbreaking work. Thousands of workers laid logs called **ties** on the ground. Heavy iron rails were then laid on the ties. Finally, long spikes were pounded into the ties to hold the rails in place. When the track had to pass through a mountain, dynamite was used to blast a hole through the rock. Many men risked their lives by blasting rock to create tunnels and passageways for the railroad.

The first steam-powered locomotive was made in England in 1804.

Linking East and West

In 1869, a cross-country railway was completed. It linked towns and cities across the United States from east to west. By 1885, Canada also had a cross-country railroad. Traveling by trans-continental railways was faster, safer, and more comfortable than making the trip in a wagon.

This 1831 locomotive was one of the first to be built in North America.

Settling new areas

The railroad played an important role in settling the western regions of both the United States and Canada. It took months to get from the east to the west by wagon, but by train it took only days. More and more people left their home in the East to start a new life in the West, where cheap land was available. People also came from other countries and made the difficult journey to these western areas.

Made in 1900, this locomotive had a cab for the engineer. It was one of the first engines to burn coal instead of wood.

Passenger trains

Early train cars were simple wooden carts with iron wheels, and the passenger cars resembled stagecoaches. As trains became more popular, bigger and better cars were built so passengers could travel more comfortably. Depending on how much they could afford, travelers chose seats in third-class, second-class, or first-class cars.

Tickets for the third-class cars were the least expensive. Passengers rested on wooden benches and bunks. There were no dining or sleeping cars in third class. Passengers ate food they had packed for the trip. Most of the passengers were people moving west to start a new life. They could not afford to pay for the more expensive tickets.

Second class

Second-class cars had cushioned seats. People could sleep in their seats or in bunks. If they paid extra, they could sleep in a separate sleeping car. Some second-class passengers brought their own food. Others got off the train to have a meal in a restaurant when the train stopped at a station to refuel.

First class

First-class tickets were the most expensive. The luxurious first-class cars had large cushioned seats. On long trips, travelers slept in sleeping cars with private beds. They ate in a dining car that served delicious meals on fine china. For first-class passengers, such as those shown below, riding the train was like taking a vacation.

Turn-of-the-century travel

As the population of towns and cities grew, new and improved roads were built. The invention of steamboats and trains made travel easier and more enjoyable. Traveling from town to town or even across the continent would soon become even faster. Which new modes of transportation did the 1900s have in store?

The first flyers

After land and water travel were no longer a challenge, people looked to the sky for faster ways of getting from place to place. The first flyers were inventors who patterned their machines after birds. To make these devices fly, they jumped off high places and hoped that their flying machines would keep them in the air. Unfortunately, most of these brave inventors experienced crash landings!

Balloons

Hot-air balloons were the first flying machines that carried people across the sky. People knew that hot air rises, so they used a flame to heat the air inside a giant balloon. Up it went, lifting a large basket that carried people inside.

Look at these early flying devices. Which one do you think had the best chance of staying in the air? If you had to invent a new way to travel, what would it be? Draw a picture of your invention.

hot-air balloon

The first cars

At the end of the 1800s, people continued to invent new ways to travel. People started riding in motor carriages, which were powered by steam engines rather than horses. These early automobiles traveled slowly and used coal for fuel. Eventually, faster engines were built, which used gasoline instead of coal.

Many people have come to see the amazing new flying machines at this fair in the early 1900s. The blimp in the right corner of the large picture is filled with a light gas called **hydrogen**, *which keeps it afloat. People are excited about the airplane that just took off. On the ground, there are some early automobiles alongside a reliable horse and carriage.*

Glossary

artisan A skilled tradesperson such as a blacksmith or carpenter

axle A shaft that rotates and, in turn, rotates a wheel that is attached to it

blaze To mark a trail by cutting trees

canal An artificial waterway dug across land through which boats can travel

convoy A large group traveling together for safety and protection

current The natural flow of a body of water that moves along a path

dugout A canoe made by hollowing out a large log

forge A fireplace in which a blacksmith heats metal

hatchet A small, short-handled ax

hull The frame of a boat

keel A long piece of wood that runs underneath a boat from the front to the rear

locomotive A steam-powered engine used to push or pull train cars

piston A solid cylinder that, using pressure created by steam or liquid, moves back and forth inside a hollow cylinder

plank A long, thick, flat piece of wood cut from a log

portage To carry a canoe over land to get from one body of water to another

runners The long metal blades of a sleigh that glide over the snow

sawmill A building where logs are sawed into planks

tarpaulin Waterproof material used to cover objects and keep them dry

ties Beams of wood that are laid across railway rails to secure them in place

wagon train A group of families traveling across a great distance in covered wagons

Index

1 2 3 4 5 6 7 8 9 0 Printed in U.S.A. 9 8 7 6 5 4 3 2 1 0